# 6 MEALS DIET COOKBOOK

A SELECTION OF THE
MOST DELICIOUS RECIPES
TO GAIN ENERGY,
LOSE WEIGHT
AND FEEL GOOD

ANNALISA WILLIAMS

# TABLE OF CONTENT

**INTRODUCTION** .................................................................................. 8

**WHAT IS 6 MEALS DIET PLAN?** ........................................................ 10

**THE BENEFITS OF 6 MEALS DIET** .................................................... 14

**LEAN AND GREEN RECIPES** ............................................................. 17
- BRAISED COLLARD GREENS IN PEANUT SAUCE WITH PORK TENDERLOIN ........ 19
- TOMATILLO AND GREEN CHILI PORK STEW .............................................. 21
- ROSEMARY CAULIFLOWER ROLLS ............................................................ 23

**FUELING RECIPES** ............................................................................. 25
- TABASCO ANZAC ....................................................................................... 27
- SWEET POTATO CASSEROLE ..................................................................... 29
- OVERNIGHT CHOCOLATE CHIA PUDDING ................................................ 31
- SLOW COOKER SAVORY BUTTERNUT SQUASH OATMEAL ....................... 32
- POLENTA WITH SEARED PEARS ................................................................ 34

**BREAKFAST** ....................................................................................... 37
- MINI ZUCCHINI BITES ............................................................................... 39
- WHOLE-WHEAT BLUEBERRY MUFFINS .................................................... 40
- LEAN AND GREEN SMOOTHIE .................................................................. 42
- MINI MAC IN A BOWL ............................................................................... 43
- ALKALINE BLUEBERRY MUFFINS ............................................................. 45
- MILLET PORRIDGE ................................................................................... 46
- JACKFRUIT VEGETABLE FRY .................................................................... 47

**MAINS** ............................................................................................... 49
- PESTO ZUCCHINI NOODLES ..................................................................... 51
- CAULIFLOWER CURRY ............................................................................. 53
- PORK AND PEPPERS CHILI ....................................................................... 54
- STEWED HERBED FRUIT .......................................................................... 55
- BOK CHOY WITH TOFU STIR FRY ............................................................ 56
- THREE-BEAN MEDLEY ............................................................................. 58
- SWEET POTATO BACON MASH ................................................................ 59

**SNACKS RECIPES** .............................................................................. 61
- CUCUMBER BITES .................................................................................... 63
- BISCUIT PIZZA .......................................................................................... 64
- STUFFED AVOCADO ................................................................................. 65
- TOMATO SALSA ........................................................................................ 66

- AVOCADO DIP ..... 67
- JALAPENO LENTIL (CHICKPEA) BURGERS + AVOCADO MANGO PICO ..... 68
- CHICKEN ENCHILADA BAKE ..... 70
- BAKED TUNA WITH ASPARAGUS ..... 72

## VEGETABLES ..... 73
- FRIED AVOCADO ..... 75
- VEGETABLES IN AIR FRYER ..... 76
- ROASTED SQUASH PUREE ..... 77
- CREAMY SPINACH AND MUSHROOM LASAGNA ..... 78
- VEGAN EDAMAME QUINOA COLLARD WRAPS ..... 80

## MEAT ..... 83
- CHICKEN STRIPS ..... 85
- CHICKEN STIR FRY ..... 86
- TOMATILLO AND GREEN CHILI PORK STEW ..... 87

## SOUPS AND STEWS ..... 89
- CREAMY CAULIFLOWER SOUP ..... 91
- CRACKPOT CHICKEN TACO SOUP ..... 92
- CAULIFLOWER SOUP ..... 93
- LIME-MINT SOUP ..... 94

## SMOOTHIES ..... 95
- BERRY PEACH SMOOTHIE ..... 97
- CANTALOUPE BLACKBERRY SMOOTHIE ..... 98
- CUCUMBER-GINGER WATER ..... 99

## DESSERTS ..... 101
- PEANUT BUTTER BROWNIE ICE CREAM SANDWICHES ..... 103
- CRANBERRY SALAD ..... 105
- CHIA PUDDING ..... 106
- AVOCADO PUDDING ..... 107
- RASPBERRY ICE CREAM ..... 108

© **Copyright 2021 by A. WILLIAMS - All rights reserved**.

The following Book is reproduced below with the goal of providing information that is as accurate and reliable as possible. Regardless, purchasing this Book can be seen as consent to the fact that both the publisher and the author of this book are in no way experts on the topics discussed within and that any recommendations or suggestions that are made herein are for entertainment purposes only.

Professionals should be consulted as needed prior to undertaking any of the action endorsed herein.

This declaration is deemed fair and valid by both the American Bar Association and the Committee of Publishers Association and is legally binding throughout the United States.

Furthermore, the transmission, duplication, or reproduction of any of the following work including specific information will be considered an illegal act irrespective of if it is done electronically or in print. This extends to creating a secondary or tertiary copy of the work or a recorded copy and is only allowed with the express written consent from the Publisher. All additional right reserved.

The information in the following pages is broadly considered a truthful and accurate account of facts and as such, any inattention, use, or misuse of the information in question by the reader will render any resulting actions solely under their purview.
There are no scenarios in which the publisher or the original author of this work can be in any fashion deemed liable for any hardship or damages that may

befall them after undertaking information described herein.

Additionally, the information in the following pages is intended only for informational purposes and should thus be thought of as universal. As befitting its nature, it is presented without assurance regarding its prolonged validity or interim quality.

Trademarks that are mentioned are done without written consent and can in no way be considered an endorsement from the trademark holder.

# INTRODUCTION

There are really numerous diet models that have sprung up in the last decade , including Dash diet, Flexible Vegan diet, Weight Watcher diet and 6 Meals diet.
These diets consist of different nutrient structures and different eating styles, each of which is effective in weight loss.

The effectiveness of 6 Meals diet has been amply demonstrated, as you can see in various journals after the results of research done by expert dieticians have been published.
These diet programs allow you to see significant changes in as little as 8 weeks and achieve your long-term health goals.

But how healthy are these fat burning diets for our bodies? Are the commercialized diets necessarily better?

One must always choose a healthy one that fits our needs. For people with special needs (such as weight loss), special diets can be used for specific periods of time and on a limited basis, but in the long run, it is important to maintain a balanced nutritional profile.

# WHAT IS 6 MEALS DIET PLAN?

If you work all day and don't have time or your kids don't leave you a spare minute and you are looking for a diet for people with little time the 6 Meals diet is one such diet plan that can help you lose weight without taking up your time.

The 6 meals diet has been pioneered by a group of expert dietician.

This Diet is low calorie and low carb and combine packaged foods with homemade meals to achieve weight loss.

The 6 meals diet involves the use of meal replacements and vegetables to cover the 6 times of the day when eating is allowed.

Diet Programs:

5 & 1

The strictest method is called 5 & 1 and it involves eating 5 meal replacements and 1 meal of protein and vegetables in order to reach an energy requirement of 800-1000 calories.

4 & 2 & 1

The 4 & 2 & 1 allows you to switch from a restricted regimen to one considered a slightly more comprehensive program by consuming 4 replacement meals, 1 meal with protein and vegetables and 1 snack.

3 & 3

The third program 3 & 3 is very similar to a maintenance diet scheme of at least 6 weeks: 3 replacement meals and 3 meals with protein and vegetables.

In order to be successful with these diet plans it is essential to introduce some rules and respect them with perseverance and commitment.

You must eat daily more or less every 2-3 hours, drink 2 liters of water, do not consume more than 200 grams of protein, exercise regularly and do not go to bed too late to wake up on time to start the next day with the right pace.

# THE BENEFITS OF 6 MEALS DIET

6 Meals a Day's Program may be a solid match for you on the off chance that you need a diet Plan that is clear and Simple to follow, that will assist you with getting in shape rapidly, and offers worked in social help.
When embarking on any new diet regimen, you may experience some difficulties along the way.
Below are the reasons why this diet regimen is considered as the easiest to follow among all commercial diet regimens.

Accomplishes Rapid Weight Loss

Most solid individuals require around 1600 to 3000 calories for each day to keep up their weight. Limiting that number to as low as 800 basically ensures weight loss for a great many people.

5&1 Plan is intended for brisk weight loss, making it a strong choice for somebody with a clinical motivation to shed Pounds quick.
You enter the fat-loss stage in just 3 days. Look for Weight loss story on YouTube to see how many people out there are losing an impressive amount of weight, even 20 or more Pounds in a week.
The average of 12 Pounds in 12 weeks on the website counts all the people that do it by themselves, and nobody knows how many times they actually follow the Plan, how many times they cheat, how much water they drink, exercise, etc.

Easy to Follow as the diet depend on generally a Prepackaged Fuels, you are only accountable for doing one meal a day on the 5&1 Plan.
Although you are encouraged to Prepare 1 to 3 green and lean foods a day, depending on your strategy, they are very simple to prepare, as the Program will include detailed recipes and a list of food options to choose from.
Also, those who don't like to cook can Purchase Packaged meals called Flavors of Home to replace Lean and Green meals.

Bundled Items Offer Comfort

5&1's shakes, soups, and all other feast substitution items are conveyed legitimately to your entryway—a degree of comfort that numerous different diets don't offer.
In spite of the fact that you should search for your own elements for "lean and green "dinners, the home conveyance choice for "Fuels" spares time and vitality. When the items show up, they're anything but difficult to get ready and make Phenomenal snatch and go suppers.

Packaged Products

They will be delivered directly at home, and they are quick-to-make and grab-and-go.

Social Support and Coaching

Health coaches are available throughout the weight loss and maintenance, stay motivated, do not cheat. Point out how people on coaching achieve a much faster and more massive weight loss.

Offers Social Help

Social help is a crucial Part of achievement with any weight loss Plan. 6 Meals training Project and gathering can give worked in consolation and backing for clients.

6 Meals Programs

Eliminates the Guesswork
You don't have to worry about what to eat all day, just cook it once a day or every other day.
Some people find that the hardest Part of the diet is the Psychological effort required to understand what to eat every day, or even every dinner.
This program reduces the Pressure of Party Planning and "running out of options" by offering customers set foods with "supplies" and rules for "simple and green" meals.
It's Not a Ketogenic Diet Carbs are allowed and higher than the majority of weight-loss diets out there, just not the refined ones.

No Counting Calories

You don't really need to count your calories when following this type of diet, just as long as you stick with the rule of Fuels, meals, snacks and water intake depending on your Preference may it be 5&1, 4&2&1 or 3&3.

# LEAN AND GREEN RECIPES

# BRAISED COLLARD GREENS IN PEANUT SAUCE WITH PORK TENDERLOIN

COOKING: 1 H 12'   PREPARATION: 20'   SERVES: 4

INGREDIENTS

- 2 cups of chicken stock
- 12 cups of chopped collard greens
- 5 tablespoons of powdered peanut butter
- 3 cloves of garlic, crushed
- 1 teaspoon of salt
- ½ teaspoon of allspice
- ½ teaspoon of black pepper
- 2 teaspoon of lemon juice
- ¾ teaspoon of hot sauce
- 1 ½ lb. of pork tenderloin

DIRECTIONS

1. Get a pot with a tight-fitting lid and combine the collards with the garlic, chicken stock, hot sauce, and half of the pepper and salt. Cook on low heat for about 1 hour or until the collards become tender.
2. Once the collards are tender, stir in the allspice, lemon juice. And powdered peanut butter. Keep warm.
3. Season the pork tenderloin with the remaining pepper and salt, and broil in a toaster oven for 10 minutes when you have an internal temperature of 1450F. Make sure to turn the tenderloin every 2 minutes to achieve an even browning all over. After

that, you can take away the pork from the oven and allow it to rest for like 5 minutes.
4.     Slice the pork as you will

NUTRITIONS: Calories: 320 Fat: 10 g Carbohydrate: 15 g Protein: 45 g

# TOMATILLO AND GREEN CHILI PORK STEW

COOKING: 20' PREPARATION: 10' SERVES: 4

INGREDIENTS

- 2 scallions, chopped
- 2 cloves of garlic
- 1 lb. tomatillos, trimmed and chopped
- 8 large romaine or green lettuce leaves, divided
- 2 serrano chilies, seeds, and membranes
- ½ tsp of dried Mexican oregano (or you can use regular oregano)
- 1 ½ lb. of boneless pork loin, to be cut into bite-sized cubes
- ¼ cup of cilantro, chopped
- ¼ tablespoon (each) salt and paper
- 1 jalapeno, seeds and membranes to be removed and thinly sliced.
- 1 cup of sliced radishes
- 4 lime wedges

DIRECTIONS

1. Combine scallions, garlic, tomatillos, 4 lettuce leaves, serrano chilies, and oregano in a blender. Then puree until smooth.
2. Put pork and tomatillo mixture in a medium pot. 1-inch of puree should cover the pork; if not, add water until it covers it. Season with pepper & salt, and cover it simmers. Simmer on heat for approximately 20 minutes.
3. Now, finely shred the remaining lettuce leaves.

4. When the stew is done cooking, garnish with cilantro, radishes, finely shredded lettuce, sliced jalapenos, and lime wedges.

Nutrition : Calories 320 Protéine 44g Carbohydrate 11g

# ROSEMARY CAULIFLOWER ROLLS

COOKING: 30' SERVES: 3

INGREDIENTS

» 1/3 cup of almond flour
» 4 cups of riced cauliflower
» 1/3 cup of reduced-fat, shredded mozzarella or cheddar cheese
» 2 eggs
» 2 tablespoons of fresh rosemary, finely chopped
» ½ teaspoon of salt

DIRECTIONS

PREPARATION: 10'

1. Preheat your oven to 4000F
2. Combine all the listed ingredients in a medium-sized bowl
3. Scoop cauliflower mixture into 12 evenly sized rolls/ biscuits onto a lightly-greased and foil-lined baking sheet.
4. Bake until it turns golden brown, which should be achieved in about 30 minutes.
5. Note: if you want to have the outside of the rolls/ biscuits crisp, then broil for some minutes before serving.

NUTRITIONS: Calories: 254 Protein: 24g Carbohydrate: 7g Fat: 8 g

# FUELING RECIPES

# TABASCO ANZAC

COOKING: 3 H 45' PREPARATION: 25' SERVES: 4

INGREDIENTS

- 85g porridge oats
- 85g desiccated coconut
- 85g sultanas
- 100g plain flour
- 100g caster sugar
- 100g butter
- 1 tbsp. golden syrup
- 2 tsp. Tabasco
- 2 tbsp. hot water
- 1 tsp. bicarbonate of soda

DIRECTIONS

1. Preheat fan assisted oven to 350F.

2. Positioned the oats, raisins, coconut, flour, and sugar in a bowl.

3. Soften the butter in a small pan and stir inside the golden syrup, Tabasco sauce, and water.

4. Add the bicarbonate of soda and mix well.

5. Add the liquid to the bowl and mix well until all the ingredients are combined.

6. Using a dessert spoon, spoon the mixture onto a but- tered baking sheet. Leave about 2.5cm in-between each spoonful to allow room for spreading.

7. Bake in batches for 8-10 minutes until golden.
8. Place the cooked biscuits onto a wire rack to cool.

NUTRITIONS: Fat: 41 g Protein: 12 g Cholesterol: 20 mg Carbohydrates: 20 g Sodium: 504mg

# SWEET POTATO CASSEROLE

COOKING: 1 H PREPARATION: 20' SERVES: 8

INGREDIENTS

- Potatoes (3 lbs., sweet, peeled, chopped)
- Greek yogurt (1 cup, nonfat)
- Cinnamon (1/2 tbsp, ground)
- Nutmeg (1/8 tsp., ground)
- Sea salt (1/4 tsp.)
- Egg whites (6 tbsp)
- Butter (1 tbsp, melted)
- Pecans (1/2 cup, chopped)
- Marshmallows (1/2 cup, miniature)
- Sugar (dash, light brown, for sprinkling)

DIRECTIONS

1. Heat your oven to 375 degrees Fahrenheit.
2. Place the potatoes (sweet) into a saucepan (large) over medium high heat.
3. Cover potatoes using water then bring to a boil, boil for approximately 30 minutes until soft.
4. Drain potatoes then place potatoes back into the saucepan.
5. Add the Greek yogurt, cinnamon (ground), nutmeg (base) and sea salt (dash) into the potatoes.
6. Stir well until coated (evenly).
7. Add in the butter (melted) and egg whites then bring to a stir once more.
8. Transfer potato mixture into a casserole dish (large).

9.   Place into oven then bake for approximately 30 minutes. Remove from heat then top with the pecans (chopped) and miniature marshmallows.
10.   Place back into oven to bake for an additional 10 minutes until marshmallows are browned.

NUTRITIONS: Protein: 2.9 g Carbohydrates: 30.1 g Dietary Fiber: 1.9 g

# OVERNIGHT CHOCOLATE CHIA PUDDING

COOKING: OVERNIGHT TO CHILL   PREPARATION: 2'
SERVES: 1

INGREDIENTS

» 1/8 cup chia seeds
» 1/2 cup unsweetened nondairy milk
» One tablespoon raw cacao powder
» 1/2 teaspoon vanilla extract
» 1/2 teaspoon pure maple syrup

DIRECTIONS

1. Stir together the chia seeds, milk, cacao powder, vanilla, and maple syrup in a large bowl. Divide be- tween 2 (1/2-pint) covered glass jars or containers. Refrigerate overnight.
2. Stir before serving.

NUTRITIONS: Calories: 213 Fat: 10g Protein: 9g Carbohydrates: 20g Fiber: 15g

# SLOW COOKER SAVORY BUTTERNUT SQUASH OATMEAL

COOKING: 6-8 H   PREPARATION: 15'   SERVES: 1

INGREDIENTS

- 1/4 cup steel-cut oats
- 1/2 cups cubed (1/2-inch pieces) peeled butternut squash (freeze any leftovers after preparing a whole squash for future meals)
- 3/4 cups of water
- 1/16 cup unsweetened nondairy milk
- 1/4 tablespoon chia seed
- 1/2 teaspoons yellow (mellow) miso paste
- 3/4 teaspoons ground ginger
- 1/4 tablespoon sesame seed, toasted
- 1/4 tablespoon chopped scallion, green parts only
- Shredded carrot, for serving (optional)

DIRECTIONS

1. In a slow cooker, combine the oats, butternut squash, and water.
2. Cover the slow cooker and cook on low for 6 to 8 hours, or until the squash is fork tender. Using a potato masher or heavy spoon, roughly mash the cooked butternut squash. Stir to combine with the oats.
3. Whisk together the milk, chia seeds, miso paste, and ginger to combine in a large bowl. Stir the mixture into the oats.

4.  Top your oatmeal bowl with sesame seeds and scallion for more plant-based fiber, top with shredded carrot (if using).

NUTRITIONS: Calories: 471 Fat: 16g Protein: 18g Carbohydrates: 69g Fiber: 53g

# POLENTA WITH SEARED PEARS

COOKING: 50'  PREPARATION: 10' SERVES: 1

INGREDIENTS

- » One cup water, divided, plus more as needed
- » 1/2 cups coarse cornmeal
- » One tablespoon pure maple syrup
- » 1/4 tablespoon molasses
- » 1/4 teaspoon ground cinnamon
- » 1/2 ripe pears, cored and diced
- » 1/4 cup fresh cranberries
- » 1/4 teaspoon chopped fresh rosemary leaves

DIRECTIONS

1. In a pan, cook 5 cups of water to a simmer.
2. While whisking continuously to avoid clumping, slowly pour in the cornmeal. Cook, often stirring with a heavy spoon, for 30 minutes. The polenta should be thick and creamy.
3. While the polenta cooks, in a saucepan over medium heat, stir together the maple syrup, molasses, the remaining 1/4 cup of water, and the cinnamon until combined. Bring it to a simmer. Add the pears and cranberries. Cook for 10 minutes, occasionally stir- ring, until the pears are tender and start to brown. Remove from the heat. Stir in the rosemary and let the mixture sit for 5 minutes. If it is too thick, add another 1/4 cup of water and re-heat.
4. Top with the cranberry-pear mixture.

NUTRITIONS: Calories: 282 Fat: 2g Protein: 4g Carbohydrates: 65g Fiber: 12g

# BREAKFAST

# MINI ZUCCHINI BITES

COOKING: 10' PREPARATION: 10' SERVES: 6

INGREDIENTS

- 1 zucchini, cut into thick circles
- 3 cherry tomatoes, halved
- 1/2 cup parmesan cheese, grated
- Salt and pepper to taste
- 1 tsp. chives, chopped

DIRECTIONS

1. Preheat the oven to 390 degrees F.
2. Add wax paper on a baking sheet.
3. Arrange the zucchini pieces.
4. Add the cherry halves on each zucchini slice.
5. Add parmesan cheese, chives, and sprinkle with salt and pepper.
6. Bake for 10 minutes. Serve.

NUTRITIONS: Fat: 1.0 g Cholesterol: 5.0 mg Sodium: 400.3 mg Potassium: 50.5 mg Carbohydrates: 7.3 g

# WHOLE-WHEAT BLUEBERRY MUFFINS

COOKING: 25' PREPARATION: 5' SERVES: 8

INGREDIENTS

- 1/2 cup plant-based milk
- 1/2 cup unsweetened applesauce
- 1/2 cup maple syrup
- 1 teaspoon vanilla extract
- 2 cups whole-wheat flour
- 1/2 teaspoon baking soda
- 1 cup blueberries

DIRECTIONS

1. Preheat the oven to 375°F.

2. In a large bowl, mix the milk, applesauce, maple syrup, and vanilla.

3. Stir in the flour and baking soda until no dry flour is left and the batter is smooth.

4. Gently fold in the blueberries until they are evenly distributed throughout the batter.

5. In a muffin tin, fill 8 muffin cups three-quarters full of batter.

6. Bake for 25 minutes, or until you can stick a knife into the center of a muffin and it comes out clean. Allow to cool before serving.

7. Tip: Both frozen and fresh blueberries will work great in this recipe. The only difference will be that

muffins using fresh blueberries will cook slightly quicker than those using frozen.

NUTRITIONS: Fat: 1 g Carbohydrates: 45 g Fiber: 2 g Protein: 4 g

# LEAN AND GREEN SMOOTHIE

COOKING: 0 PREPARATION: 2' SERVES: 1

INGREDIENTS

- Six kale leaves
- Two peeled oranges
- 2 cups of mango kombucha
- 2 cups of chopped pineapple
- 2 cups of water

DIRECTIONS

1. Break up the oranges, place in the blender,
2. Add the mango kombucha, chopped pineapple, and kale leaves into the blender
3. Blend everything until it is smooth.
4. Smoothie is ready to be taken.

NUTRITIONS : Calories : 81 Protéine: 2 g Carbohydrates: 19 g Fats: 1 g

# MINI MAC IN A BOWL

COOKING: 15' PREPARATION: 5' SERVES: 1

INGREDIENTS

- 5 ounce of lean ground beef
- Two tablespoons of diced white or yellow onion.
- 1/8 teaspoon of onion powder
- 1/8 teaspoon of white vinegar
- 1 ounce of dill pickle slices
- One teaspoon sesame seed
- 3 cups of shredded Romaine lettuce
- Cooking spray
- Two tablespoons reduced-fat shredded cheddar cheese
- Two tablespoons of Wish-bone light thousand island as dressing

DIRECTIONS

1. Place a lightly greased small skillet on fire to heat,
2. Add your onion to cook for about 2-3 minutes,
3. Next, add the beef and allow cooking until it's brown
4. Next, mix your vinegar and onion powder with the dressing,
5. Finally, top the lettuce with the cooked meat and sprinkle cheese on it, add your pickle slices.
6. Drizzle the mixture with the sauce and sprinkle the sesame seeds also.

7. Your mini mac in a bowl is ready for consumption.

NUTRITIONS : Calories : 150 Protéin: 21 g
Carbohydrates: 32 g  Fat : 19 g

# ALKALINE BLUEBERRY MUFFINS

COOKING: 20' PREPARATION: 5' SERVES: 3

INGREDIENTS

- 1 cup Coconut Milk
- 3/4 cup Spelt Flour
- 3/4 Teff Flour
- 1/2 cup Blueberries
- 1/3 cup Agave
- 1/4 cup Sea Moss Gel
- 1/2 tsp. Sea Salt
- Grapeseed Oil

DIRECTIONS

1. Adjust the temperature of the oven to 365 degrees.
2. Grease 6 regular-size muffin cups with muffin liners.
3. In a bowl, mix together sea salt, sea moss, agave, coconut milk, and flour gel until they are properly blended.
4. You then crimp in blueberries.
5. Coat the muffin pan lightly with the grapeseed oil.
6. Pour in the muffin batter.
7. Bake for at least 30 minutes until it turns golden brown.
8. Serve.

NUTRITIONS: Calories: 160 kcal Fat: 5g Carbs: 25g Proteins: 2g

# MILLET PORRIDGE

COOKING: 20' PREPARATION: 10' SERVES: 2

INGREDIENTS

- Sea salt
- 1 tbsp. finely chopped coconuts
- 1/2 cup unsweetened coconut milk
- 1/2 cup rinsed and drained millet
- 1-1/2 cups alkaline water
- 3 drops liquid stevia

DIRECTIONS

1. Sauté the millet in a non-stick skillet for about 3 minutes.
2. Add salt and water then stir.
3. Let the meal boil then reduce the amount of heat.
4. Cook for 15 minutes then add the remaining ingredients. Stir.
5. Cook the meal for 4 extra minutes.
6. Serve the meal with toping of the chopped nuts.

NUTRITIONS: Calories: 219 kcal Fat: 4.5g Carbs: 38.2g Protein: 6.4g

# JACKFRUIT VEGETABLE FRY

COOKING: 5' PREPARATION: 5' SERVES: 6

INGREDIENTS

- 2 finely chopped small onions
- 2 cups finely chopped cherry tomatoes
- 1/8 tsp. ground turmeric
- 1 tbsp. olive oil
- 2 seeded and chopped red bell peppers
- 3 cups seeded and chopped firm jackfruit
- 1/8 tsp. cayenne pepper
- 2 tbsps. chopped fresh basil leaves
- Salt

DIRECTIONS

1. In a greased skillet, sauté the onions and bell pep- pers for about 5 minutes.
2. Add the tomatoes then stir.
3. Cook for 2 minutes.
4. Then add the jackfruit, cayenne pepper, salt, and turmeric.
5. Cook for about 8 minutes.
6. Garnish the meal with basil leaves.
7. Serve warm.

NUTRITIONS: Calories: 236 kcal Fat: 1.8g Carbs: 48.3g Protein:

# MAINS

# PESTO ZUCCHINI NOODLES

COOKING: 30' PREPARATION: 10' SERVES: 4

INGREDIENTS

- 4 zucchinis, spiralized
- 1 tbsp avocado oil
- 2 garlic cloves, chopped
- 2/3 cup olive oil
- 1/3 cup parmesan cheese, grated
- 2 cups fresh basil
- 1/3 cup almonds
- 1/8 tsp. black pepper
- 3/4 tsp. sea salt

DIRECTIONS

1. Add zucchini noodles into a colander and sprinkle with 1/4 teaspoon of salt.
2. Cover and let sit for 30 minutes.
3. Drain zucchini noodles well and pat dry.
4. Preheat the oven to 400 F.
5. Place almonds on a parchment-lined baking sheet and bake for 6-8 minutes.
6. Transfer toasted almonds into the food processor and process until coarse.
7. Add olive oil, cheese, basil, garlic, pepper, and re- maining salt in a food processor with almonds and process until pesto texture.
8. Heat avocado oil in a large pan over medium-high heat.
9. Add zucchini noodles and cook for 4-5 minutes.

10. Pour pesto over zucchini noodles, mix well and cook for 1 minute.
11. Serve immediately with baked salmon.

NUTRITIONS: Calories: 525 Cal Fat: 47.4 g Carbohydrates: 9.3 g Sugar: 3.8 g Protein:16.6 g Cholesterol: 30 mg

# CAULIFLOWER CURRY

COOKING: 5H PREPARATION: 5' SERVES: 4

INGREDIENTS

- 1 cauliflower head, florets separated
- 2 carrots, sliced
- 1 red onion, chopped
- ¾ cup coconut milk
- 2 garlic cloves, minced
- 2 tablespoons curry powder
- A pinch of salt and black pepper
- 1 tablespoon red pepper flakes
- 1 teaspoon garam masala

DIRECTIONS

1. In your slow cooker, mix all the ingredients.
2. Cover, cook on high for 5 hours, divide into bowls
and serve.

NUTRITIONS: Calories: 160 Fat: 11.5g Fiber: 5.4g Carbs: 14.7g Protein: 3.6g

# PORK AND PEPPERS CHILI

COOKING: 8H 5' PREPARATION: 5' SERVES: 4

INGREDIENTS

- » 1 red onion, chopped
- » 2 pounds' pork, ground
- » 4 garlic cloves, minced
- » 2 red bell peppers, chopped
- » 1 celery stalk, chopped
- » 25 ounces' fresh tomatoes, peeled, crushed
- » ¼ cup green chilies, chopped
- » 2 tablespoons fresh oregano, chopped
- » 2 tablespoons chili powder
- » A pinch of salt and black pepper
- » A drizzle of olive oil

DIRECTIONS

1. Heat up a sauté pan with the oil over medium-high heat and add the onion, garlic and the meat. Mix and brown for 5 minutes then transfer to your slow cooker.
2. Add the rest of the ingredients, toss, cover and cook
on low for 8 hours.
3. Divide everything into bowls and serve.

NUTRITIONS: Calories: 448 Fat: 13g Fiber: 6.6g Carbs: 20.2g Protein: 63g

# STEWED HERBED FRUIT

COOKING: 6-8H PREPARATION: 15' SERVES: 12

INGREDIENTS

- 2 cups dried apricots
- 2 cups prunes
- 2 cups dried unsulfured pears
- 2 cups dried apples
- 1 cup dried cranberries
- 1/4 cup honey
- 6 cups water
- 1 teaspoon dried thyme leaves
- 1 teaspoon dried basil leaves

DIRECTIONS

1. In a 6-quart slow cooker, mix all of the ingredients.
2. Cover and cook on low for 6 to 8 hours, or until the fruits have absorbed the liquid and are tender.
3. Store in the refrigerator up to 1 week.
4. You can freeze the fruit in 1-cup portions for more extended storage.

NUTRITIONS: Calories: 242 Cal Carbohydrates: 61 g Sugar: 43 g Fiber: 9 g Fat: 0 g Saturated Fat: 0 g Protein: 2 g Sodium: 11 mg

# BOK CHOY WITH TOFU STIR FRY

COOKING: 15' PREPARATION: 15' SERVES: 4

INGREDIENTS

- » Super-firm tofu; 1 lb. (drained and pressed)
- » Coconut oil; one tablespoon
- » Clove of garlic; 1 (minced)
- » Baby bok choy; 3 heads (chopped)
- » Low-sodium vegetable broth;
- » Maple syrup; 2 teaspoons
- » Braggs liquid aminos
- » Sambal oelek; 1 to 2 teaspoons (similar chili sauce)
- » Scallion or green onion; 1 (chopped)
- » Freshly grated ginger; 1 teaspoon
- » Quinoa/rice, for serving

DIRECTIONS

1. With paper towels, Pat pressed the tofu dry and cut
into tiny pieces of bite-size around 1/2 inch wide.
2. Heat coconut oil in a wide skillet onto a warm.
3. Remove tofu and stir-fry until painted softly.
4. Stir-fry for 1-2 minutes, before the choy of the Bok,
starts to wilt.
5. When this occurs, you'll want to apply the vegetable broth and all the remaining ingredients to the skillet.
6. Hold the mixture stir-frying until all components are well coated, and the bulk of the liquid evaporates, around 5-6 min.

7. Serve over brown rice or quinoa.

NUTRITIONS: Calories: 263.7 Cal Fat 4.2 g Cholesterol: 0.3 mg Sodium: 683.6 mg Potassium: 313.7 mg Carbohydrate: 35.7 g

# THREE-BEAN MEDLEY

COOKING: 6-8H PREPARATION: 15' SERVES: 8

INGREDIENTS

» 11/4 cups dried kidney beans, rinsed and drained
» 11/4 cups dried black beans, rinsed and drained
» 11/4 cups dried black-eyed peas, rinsed and drained
» 1 onion, chopped
» 1 leek, chopped
» 2 garlic cloves, minced
» 2 carrots, peeled and chopped
» 6 cups low-sodium vegetable broth
» 11/2 cups water
» 1/2 teaspoon dried thyme leaves

DIRECTIONS

1. In a 6-quart slow cooker, mix all of the ingredients.
2. Cover and cook on low for 6 to 8 hours, or until the
beans are tender and the liquid is absorbed.

NUTRITIONS: Calories: 284 Cal Carbohydrates: 56 g Sugar: 6 g Fiber: 19 g Fat: 0 g Satu- rated Fat: 0 g Protein: 1 9g Sodium: 131 mg

# SWEET POTATO BACON MASH

COOKING: 20' PREPARATION: 10 'SERVES: 4

INGREDIENTS

- 3 sweet potatoes, peeled
- 4 oz. bacon, chopped
- 1 cup chicken stock
- 1 tablespoon butter
- 1 teaspoon salt
- 2 oz. Parmesan, grated

DIRECTIONS

1. Dice sweet potato and put it in the pan.
2. Add chicken stock and close the lid.
3. Boil the vegetables for until they are soft.
4. After this, drain the chicken stock.
5. Mash the sweet potato with the help of the potato masher. Add grated cheese and butter.
6. Mix up together salt and chopped bacon. Fry the mixture until it is crunchy (10-15 minutes).
7. Add cooked bacon in the mashed sweet potato and mix up with the help of the spoon.
8. It is recommended to serve the meal warm or hot.

NUTRITIONS: Calories: 304 Fat: 18.1 Fiber: 2.9 Carbs: 18.8 Protein: 17

# SNACKS RECIPES

# CUCUMBER BITES

COOKING: 0' PREPARATION: 10' SERVES: 12

INGREDIENTS

- 1 English cucumber, sliced into 32 rounds
- 10 ounces hummus
- 16 cherry tomatoes, halved
- 1 tablespoon parsley, chopped
- 1 ounce feta cheese, crumbled

DIRECTIONS

1. Spread the hummus on each cucumber round, divide the tomato halves on each, sprinkle the cheese and parsley on to and serve as an appetizer.

NUTRITIONS: Calories 162 Fat 3.4 g Fiber 2 g Carbs 6.4 g Protein 2.4 g

# BISCUIT PIZZA

COOKING: 15' PREPARATION: 5' SERVES: 2

INGREDIENTS

» 1 sachet Buttermilk Cheddar and Herb Biscuit
» 2 tablespoons water
» 1 tablespoon tomato sauce
» 1 tablespoon low fat cheese, shredded

DIRECTIONS

1. Preheat the oven or toaster to 3500F for 5 minutes.
2. In a bowl, stir the Buttermilk Cheddar and Herb Biscuit with water to form a thick paste. Spread into a thin circle on a baking tray lined with parchment paper.
3. Cook for 10 minutes to harden.
4. Once harden, spread tomato sauce on top and cheese.
5. Bake for another 5 minutes.

NUTRITIONS: Calories per serving: 437 Cal Protein: 9.5 g Carbohydrates: 68.5 g Fat: 5.3 g Sugar: 4.3 g

# STUFFED AVOCADO

COOKING: 0' PREPARATION: 10' SERVES: 2

INGREDIENTS

- 1 avocado, halved and pitted
- 10 ounces canned tuna, drained
- 2 tablespoons sun-dried tomatoes, chopped
- 1 and ½ tablespoon basil pesto
- 2 tablespoons black olives, pitted and chopped
- Salt and black pepper to the taste
- 2 teaspoons pine nuts, toasted and chopped
- 1 tablespoon basil, chopped

DIRECTIONS

1. Combine the tuna with the sun-dried tomatoes in a bowl, and the rest of the ingredients except the avocado and stir.
2. Stuff the avocado halves with the tuna mix and serve as an appetizer.

NUTRITIONS: Calories 233 Fat 9 g Fiber 2 g Carbs 11.4 g Protein 6.5 g

# TOMATO SALSA

PREPARATION: 5'

INGREDIENTS

- 1 garlic clove, minced   1.
- 4 tablespoons olive oil
- 5 tomatoes, cubed
- 1 tablespoon balsamic vinegar
- ¼ cup basil, chopped
- 1 tablespoon parsley, chopped
- 1 tablespoon chives, chopped
- Salt and black pepper to the taste
- Pita chips for serving

DIRECTIONS

Mix the tomatoes with the garlic in a bowl, and the rest of the ingredients except the pita chips, stir, divide into small cups and serve with the pita chips on the side.

NUTRITIONS: Calories 160 Fat 13.7 g Fiber 5.5 g Carbs 10.1 g Protein 2.2

# AVOCADO DIP

COOKING: 0' PREPARATION: 5'

INGREDIENTS
- ½ cup heavy cream    1.
- 1 green chili pepper, chopped
- Salt and pepper to the taste
- 4 avocados, pitted, peeled and chopped
- 1 cup cilantro, chopped
- ¼ cup lime juice

DIRECTIONS

Pour the cream with the avocados and the rest of the ingredients in a blender, and pulse well. Divide the mix into bowls and serve cold as a party dip.

NUTRITIONS: Calories 200 Fat 14.5 g Fiber 3.8 g Carbs 8.1 gProtein7.6g

# JALAPENO LENTIL (CHICKPEA) BURGERS + AVOCADO MANGO PICO

COOKING: 10'     PREPARATION: 15'     SERVES: 5

INGREDIENTS

- Dried red lentils; half cup; rinsed
- Chickpeas; 1 to 12 ounces can; rinsed
- Ground cumin; one teaspoon
- Chili powder; one teaspoon
- Sea salt; one teaspoon
- Packed cilantro; half cup
- Garlic cloves minced
- Jalapeno finely chopped
- Red onion; half, small; minced
- Red bell pepper
- Carrot; shredded
- Oat bran/oat flour; 1/4 cup (gluten-free)
- Lettuce/hamburger buns
- For Pico:
- Ripe mango (1) diced
- Ripe avocado (1) diced
- Red onion; half, small;
- finely diced Chopped cilantro;
- half cup Fresh lime juice;
- half teaspoon Sea salt

DIRECTIONS

1. Put all ingredients in a large bowl and mix.
2. Stir in the salt to compare.
3. Put a medium saucepan on medium heat, add lentils plus 1 1/2 cups of water, then bring water to a

boil, cover it afterward, lower the heat to low, and then simmer lentils until the water is absorbed.
4. Drain, and set aside some extra water.
5. In a food processor, put the cooked lentils, chick- peas, garlic, sea salt, cilantro, chili powder and cum- in, and blend until the beans and lentils are smooth.
6. Add tomato, red pepper, jalapeno, and carrot to compare.
7. Divide into 6 equal parts and use your hands to create dense patties.
8. Heat skillet over a medium-high flame; apply 1/2
tablespoon of olive oil
9. Place a few burgers in at a time and cook on either side for a couple of minutes, just until crisp and golden brown.
10. Repeat with remaining patties and add olive oil whenever desired.
11. Place the patties in a bun or lettuce and finish with mango avocado pico.

NUTRITIONS : Carbohydrates: 34.9 g Calories: 225 Cal Sugar: 7.7 g Fats: 6.1 g

# CHICKEN ENCHILADA BAKE

COOKING: 50' PREPARATION: 20' SERVES: 5

INGREDIENTS

» 5 oz. shredded chicken breast (I boil and shred ahead) or 99 percent fat free White Chicken can be used in a pan.
» 1- Can paste Tomatoes
» 1 – Low sodium chicken broth can be fat free.
» 1/4 cup-cheese with low fat mozzarella
» 1 Tablespoon -oil
» 1-tbsp of salt
» Ground cumin, chili powder, garlic powder, oregano and onion powder (all to taste).
» 1 to 2 Zucchini sliced long ways (similar to lasagna noodles) into thin lines.
» Sliced (Optional) olives.

DIRECTIONS

1. Prepare Enchilada Sauce: add olive oil in sauce pan over medium / high heat, stir in tomato paste and seasonings, and heat in chicken broth for 2-3 min.
2. Stirring regularly to boil, turn heat to low for 15 min.
3. Set aside & Cool to ambient temperature.
4. Pull-strip of Zucchini through enchilada sauce and lay flat on the pan's bot- tom in a small baking pan (88) spray with Pam.
5. Next add the chicken a little less than 1/4 cup of enchilada sauce and mix it.

6. Attach chicken to the covers end to end of the baking tray.
7. Sprinkle over chicken with some bacon.
8. Add another layer of the pulled zucchini via enchilada sauce (similar to lasagna making).
9. When needed, cover with the remaining cheese and olives on top. Bake for 35 to 40 minutes.
10. Keep an eye on them.
11. When the cheese begins burning cover with foil.

NUTRITIONS: Calories: 312 Cal Carbohydrates: 21.3 g Protein: 27 g Fat: 10.2 g

# BAKED TUNA WITH ASPARAGUS

COOKING: 10' PREPARATION: 10' SERVES: 2

INGREDIENTS

- 2 tuna steak
- 1 cup asparagus, trimmed
- 1 tsp. almond butter
- 1 tsp. rosemary
- 1/2 tsp. oregano
- 1/2 tsp. garlic powder
- 1tsp lemon juice
- 1/2 tsp. ginger powder
- 1 tbsp olive oil
- 1 tsp. red chili powder
- Salt and pepper to taste

DIRECTIONS

1. Marinate the tuna using oregano, lemon juice, salt, pepper, red chili powder, garlic, ginger, and let it sit for 10 minutes.
2. In a pan, add the olive oil.
3. Fry the tuna steaks 2 minutes per side.
4. In another pan, melt the almond butter.
5. Toss the asparagus with salt, pepper, and rosemary for 3 minutes.
6. Serve.

NUTRITIONS: Fat: 4.7 g Cholesterol: 0.0 mg Sodium: 98.5 mg Potassium: 171.6 mg Carbo- hydrate: 3.2 g

# VEGETABLES

# FRIED AVOCADO

COOKING: 10' PREPARATION: 15' SERVES: 2

INGREDIENTS

- 2 avocados cut into wedges 25 mm thick
- 50g Pan crumbs bread
- 2g garlic powder
- 2g onion powder
- 1g smoked paprika
- 1g cayenne pepper
- Salt and pepper to taste
- 60g all-purpose flour
- 2 eggs, beaten
- Nonstick Spray Oil
- Tomato sauce or ranch sauce, to serve

DIRECTIONS

1. Cut the avocados into 25 mm thick pieces.
2. Combine the crumbs, garlic powder, onion powder, smoked paprika, cayenne pepper and salt in a bowl.
3. Separate each wedge of avocado in the flour, then dip the beaten eggs and stir in the breadcrumb mixture.
4. Preheat the air fryer.
5. Place the avocados in the preheated air fryer baskets, spray with oil spray and cook at 205°C for 10 minutes. Turn the fried avocado halfway through cooking and sprinkle with cooking oil.
6. Serve with tomato sauce or ranch sauce.

NUTRITIONS: Calories: 123 Carbs: 2 g Fat: 11 g Protein: 4 g

# VEGETABLES IN AIR FRYER

PREPARATION: 20' SERVES: 2 COOKING: 30'

INGREDIENTS

- 2 potatoes
- 1 zucchini
- 1 onion
- 1 red pepper
- 1 green pepper

DIRECTIONS

1. Cut the potatoes into slices.
2. Cut the onion into rings.
3. Cut the zucchini slices
4. Cut the peppers into strips.
5. Put all the ingredients in the bowl and add a little salt, ground pepper and some extra virgin olive oil.
6. Mix well.
7. Pass to the basket of the air fryer.
8. Select 1600C, 30 minutes.
9. Check that the vegetables are to your liking.
10. Ladle soup into bowls and serve.

NUTRITIONS: Calories: 133 Carbs: 2 g Fat: 11 g Protein: 4 g Fiber: 0,5g

# ROASTED SQUASH PUREE

COOKING: 7 H PREPARATION: 20' SERVES: 8

INGREDIENTS

» 1 (3-pound) butternut squash, peeled, seeded, and cut into 1-inch pieces
» 3 (1-pound) acorn squash, peeled, seeded, and cut
into 1-inch pieces
» 2 onions, chopped
» 3 garlic cloves, minced
» 2 tablespoons olive oil
» 1 teaspoon dried marjoram leaves
» 1/2 teaspoon salt
» 1/8 teaspoon freshly ground black pepper

DIRECTIONS

1. In a 6-quart slow cooker, mix all of the ingredients.
2. Cover and cook on low for 6 to 7 hours, or until the
squash is tender when pierced with a fork.
3. Use a potato masher to mash the squash right in the slow cooker.

NUTRITIONS: Calories: 175 Cal Carbohydrates: 38 g Sugar: 1 g Fiber: 3 g Fat: 4 g Saturated Fat: 1 g Protein: 3 g Sodium: 149 mg

# CREAMY SPINACH AND MUSHROOM LASAGNA

COOKING: 20' PREPARATION: 60' SERVES: 6

INGREDIENTS

- 10 lasagna noodles
- 1 package whole milk ricotta
- 2 packages of frozen chopped spinach.
- 4 cups mozzarella cheese (divided and shredded)
- 3/4 cup grated fresh Parmesan
- 3 tablespoons chopped fresh parsley leaves(optional)
- For the Sauce:
- 1/4 cup 0f butter(unsalted)
- 2 cloves garlic
- 1 pound of thinly sliced cremini mushroom
- 1 diced onion
- 1/4 cup flour
- 4 cups milk, kept at room temperature
- 1 teaspoon basil(dried)
- Pinch of nutmeg
- Salt and freshly ground black pepper, to taste.

DIRECTIONS

1. Preheat oven to 352 degrees F.
2. To make the sauce, over a medium portion of heat, melt your butter, Add garlic, mushrooms and

onion. Cook and stir at intervals until it becomes tender at about 3-4 minutes.

3. Whisk in flour until lightly browned, it takes about 1 minute for it to become brown.

4. Next, whisk in the milk gradually, and cook, whisking always, about 2-3 minute till it becomes thickened. Stir in basil, oregano and nutmeg, sea- son with salt and pepper for taste.

5. Then set aside.

6. In another pot of boiling salted water, cook lasagna noodles according to the package instructions.

7. Spread 1 cup mushroom sauce onto the bottom of a baking dish; top it with 4 lasagna noodles, 1/2 of the spinach, 1 cup mozzarella cheese and 1/4 cup Parmesan.

8. Repeat this process with remaining noodles, mushroom sauce and cheeses.

9. Place into oven and bake for 35-45 minutes, or until it starts bubbling. Then boil for 2-3 minutes until it becomes brown and translucent.

10. Let cool 15 minutes.

11. Serve it with garnished parsley (Optional)

NUTRITIONS: Calories: 488.3 Cal Fats: 19.3 g Cholesterol: 88.4 mg Sodium: 451.9 mg Carbohydrates: 51.0 g Dietary Fiber: 7.0 g Protein: 25.0 g

# VEGAN EDAMAME QUINOA COLLARD WRAPS

COOKING: 15' PREPARATION: 5' SERVES: 4

INGREDIENTS
- For the wrap:
- Collard leaves; 2 to 3
- Grated carrot; 1/4 cup
- Sliced cucumber; 1/4 cup
- Red bell pepper; 1/4; thin strips
- Orange bell pepper; 1/4; thin strips
- Cooked quinoa; 1/3 cup
- Shelled defrosted edamame; 1/3 cup
- For the dressing:
- Fresh ginger root; 3 tablespoons; peeled + chopped
- Cooked chickpeas; 1 cup
- Clove of garlic; 1
- Rice vinegar; 4 tablespoons
- Low sodium tamari/coconut aminos; 2 tablespoons
- Lime juice; 2 tablespoons
- Water; 1/4 cup
- Few pinches of chili flakes
- Stevia; 1 pack

DIRECTIONS

1. For the dressing, combine all the ingredients and purée in a food processor until smooth.
2. Load into a little jar or tub, and set aside.
3. Place the collar leaves on a flat surface, covering one another to create a tighter tie.
4. Take 1 tablespoon of ginger dressing and blend it up with the prepared quinoa.

5.   Spoon the prepared quinoa onto the leaves and shape a simple horizontal line at the closest end.
6.   Supplement with the edamame with all the veggie fillings left over.
7.   Drizzle around 1 tablespoon of the ginger dressing
on top, then fold the cover's sides inwards.
8.   Pullover the fillings the side of the cover closest to
you, then turn the whole body away to seal it up.

NUTRITIONS: Calories: 295 Cal Sugar: 3 g Sodium: 200 mg Fat: 13 g

# MEAT

## CHICKEN STRIPS

COOKING: 50' PREPARATION: 10'SERVES: 3

INGREDIENTS

- 1 Snack Cracker Pack
- 6 Ounces breast, cut into strips
- 2 Pockets. Walden Farms Dressing Salad, every taste

DIRECTIONS

1. Preheat oven to 350 ° C. Pulse 1 packet of Snack Crackers in a food processor.
2. These must be pulsed into excellent crumbs.
3. Dip chicken SEED gently into dressing for Walden Farms Salad.
4. Shake off overdressing.
5. In essence, you just want to get the chicken wet so that the crumbs can stick to them.
6. Press the strips of chicken over the crumbs.
7. Take your time and get sweet, coated chicken.
8. Then spray Pam or some other non-stick cooking spray to a baking sheet.
9. Place the chicken on the sheet and bake within 30- 40 minutes.

NUTRITIONS: Fat: 25.7 g Fiber: 2.2 g Protein: 35.4 g

# CHICKEN STIR FRY

COOKING: 10' PREPARATION: 10' SERVES: 2

INGREDIENTS

- Boneless and skinless breast of chicken
- I cup each of chopped red bell pepper and green bell pepper
- 1 cup of broccoli slaw
- I teaspoon of crushed red pepper
- 1/2 cup of chicken broth
- 2 tablespoon soy sauce

DIRECTIONS

1. Add chopped red and green bell pepper into the chicken broth, add the broccoli slaw also.
2. Next, add your soy sauce, red pepper, and the bone- less chicken (shredded).
3. Stir and allow to cook for a few minutes, do this until
the peppers are tender, and your delicacy is ready.

NUTRITIONS: Calories 137.0 Cal Fats 1.2 g Cholesterol: 27.5 mg Sodium: 873.4 mg Total Carbs: 15.4 g Dietary Fiber: 7.0 g Protein: 15.1g

# TOMATILLO AND GREEN CHILI PORK STEW

COOKING: 45' PREPARATION: 15' SERVES: 4

INGREDIENTS

- 2 scallions, chopped
- 2 cloves of garlic
- 1 lb. tomatillos, trimmed and chopped
- 8 large romaine or green lettuce leaves, divided
- 2 Serrano chilies, seeds, and membranes
- 1/2 tsp. of dried Mexican oregano (or you can use regular oregano)
- 1 1/2 lb. of boneless pork loin, to be cut into bite-sized cubes
- 1/4 cup of cilantro, chopped
- 1/4 tablespoon (each) salt and paper
- 1 jalapeno, seeds and membranes to be removed and thinly sliced.
- 1 cup of sliced radishes
- 4 lime wedges

DIRECTIONS

1. Combine scallions, garlic, tomatillos, 4 lettuce leaves, Serrano chilies, and oregano in a blender.
2. Then puree until smooth.
3. Put pork and tomatillo mixture in a medium pot. 1-inch of puree should cover the pork; if not, add water until it covers it.
4. Season with pepper & salt, and cover it simmers.

5. Simmer on low heat for approximately 20 minutes.
6. Now, finely shred the remaining lettuce leaves.
7. When the stew is done cooking, garnish with cilantro, radishes, finely shredded lettuce, sliced jalapenos, and lime wedges.

NUTRITIONS: Calories: 370 Cal Proteins: 36 g Carbohydrates: 14 g Fat: 19 g

# SOUPS AND STEWS

# CREAMY CAULIFLOWER SOUP

COOKING: 30' PREPARATION: 15' SERVES: 6

INGREDIENTS

- 5 cups cauliflower rice
- 8 oz. cheddar cheese, grated
- 2 cups unsweetened almond milk
- 2 cups vegetable stock
- 2 tbsp water
- 1 small onion, chopped
- 2 garlic cloves, minced
- 1 tbsp olive oil
- Pepper & Salt

DIRECTIONS

1. Heat olive oil in a large stockpot over medium heat.
2. Add onion and garlic and cook for 1-2 minutes. Add cauliflower rice and water.
3. Cover and cook for 5-7 minutes.
4. Add vegetable stock and almond milk and stir.
5. Bring to boil.
6. Turn heat to low and simmer for 5 minutes.
7. Turn off the heat.
8. Slowly add cheddar cheese and stir until smooth.
9. Season soup with pepper and salt.
10. Stir well and serve hot.

NUTRITIONS: Calories: 214 Cal Fat: 16.5 g Carbohydrates: 7.3 g Sugar: 3 g Protein: 11.6 g Cholesterol: 40 mg

# CRACKPOT CHICKEN TACO SOUP

COOKING: 6H PREPARATION: 15' SERVES: 6

INGREDIENTS

- » 2 frozen boneless chicken breasts
- » 2 cans of white beans or black beans
- » 1 can of diced tomatoes
- » Green chili's
- » 1/2 onion chopped
- » 1/2 packet of taco seasoning
- » 1/2 teaspoon of Garlic salt
- » 1 cup of chicken broth
- » Salt and pepper to taste
- » Tortilla chips, cheese sour cream and cilantro as toppings, as well as chili pepper (this is optional).

DIRECTIONS

1. Put your frozen chicken into the crock pot and place the other ingredients into the pool too.
2. Leave to cook for about 6-8 hours.
3. After cooking, take out the chicken and shred to the size you want.
4. Finally, place the shredded chicken into the crockpot and put it on a slow cooker. Stir and allow to cook.
5. You can add more beans and tomatoes also to help stretch the meat and make it tastier.

NUTRITIONS: Carbohydrates: 47 g Protein: 29 g Fat: 4 g Cholesterol: 48 mg Sodium: 1071 mg Fiber: 12 g

## CAULIFLOWER SOUP

COOKING: 20' PREPARATION: 5' SERVES: 4

INGREDIENTS

- 2 cup cauliflower florets, diced
- 1 cup heavy cream
- 2 cup vegetable stock
- 1 tbsp chives, minced
- Salt and pepper to taste
- 1 garlic clove, minced
- 1 tbsp almond butter

DIRECTIONS

1. In a large saucepan, add the almond butter.
2. Toss the garlic until it turns golden.
3. Add the cauliflower and toss for 2 minutes.
4. Add the vegetable stock and cook on high heat for 10 minutes.
5. Add the heavy cream, chives, salt, pepper, and cook for 8 minutes.
6. Serve hot.

NUTRITIONS: Fat: 5.5 g Cholesterol: 4.6 mg Sodium: 408 mg Potassium: 418 mg Carbohydrates: 16 g

# LIME-MINT SOUP

COOKING: 20' PREPARATION: 5' SERVES: 4

INGREDIENTS

- 4 cups vegetable broth
- 1/4 cup fresh mint leaves, roughly chopped
- 1/4 cup chopped scallions, white and green parts
- 3 garlic cloves, minced
- 3 tablespoons freshly squeezed lime juice

DIRECTIONS

1. In a large stockpot, combine the broth, mint, scallions, garlic, and lime juice.
2. Bring to a boil over medium-high heat.
3. Cover, reduce the heat to low, simmer for 15 minutes, and serve.

NUTRITIONS: Fat: 2 g Carbohydrates: 5 g Fiber: 1 g Protein: 5 g

# SMOOTHIES

# BERRY PEACH SMOOTHIE

COOKING: 5' PREPARATION: 5'SERVES: 2

INGREDIENTS

- 1 cup coconut water
- 1 tbsp hemp seeds
- 1 tbsp agave
- ½ cup strawberries
- ½ cup blueberries
- ½ cup cherries
- ½ cup peaches

DIRECTIONS

1. Toss all your ingredients into your blender then process till smooth and creamy.
2. Serve immediately and enjoy.

NUTRITIONS: Calories: 117 Fat: 2.5g Carbs: 22.5g Protein: 3.5g

# CANTALOUPE BLACKBERRY SMOOTHIE

COOKING: 5' PREPARATION: 5' SERVES: 2

INGREDIENTS

- 1 cup coconut milk yogurt
- ½ cup blackberries
- 2 cups fresh cantaloupe
- 1 banana

DIRECTIONS

1. Toss all your ingredients into your blender then process till smooth.
2. Serve and enjoy.

NUTRITIONS: Calories: 103 Fat: 0.5g Carbs: 4.2.g Protein: 1.5g

# CUCUMBER-GINGER WATER

COOKING: 5' PREPARATION: 5' SERVES: 2

INGREDIENTS

- 1 sliced Cucumber
- 1 smashed thumb of Ginger Root
- 2 cups of Spring Water

DIRECTIONS

1. Prepare and put all ingredients in a jar with a lid.
2. Let the water infuse overnight. Store it in the refrigerator.
3. Serve and enjoy your Cucumber-Ginger Water throughout the day!

NUTRITIONS: Calories: 117 Fat: 2g Carbs: 6.2.g Protein: 9.5g Fiber 2g

# DESSERTS

# PEANUT BUTTER BROWNIE ICE CREAM SANDWICHES

COOKING: 2' PREPARATION: 2' SERVES: 2

INGREDIENTS

» 1 packet Brownie Mix
» 3 tablespoons water
» 1 Peanut Butter Crunch Bar or any bar of your choice
» 2 tablespoons Peanut Butter Powder
» 1 tablespoon water
» 2 tablespoons cool whip

DIRECTIONS

1. Melt the Brownie Mix with water.
2. Add in the Peanut Butter Crunch until a dough is formed.
3. Spoon 4 dough balls on a plate and flatten using the palm of your hands.
4. Make sure that the dough is 1/4 inch thick.
5. Place in a microwave oven and cook for 2 minutes.
6. Meanwhile, mix the Peanut Butter Powder and water to form a paste.
7. Add cool whip. Set aside in the fridge to chill for at least 1 hour.
8. Take the cookies out from the microwave oven and allow to cool.
9. Once cooled, spoon the Peanut Butter ice cream in between two cookies.

10.   Serve immediately.

NUTRITIONS: Calories per serving: 410 Cal Protein: 8.3 g Carbohydrates: 57.6 g Fat: 13.2 g Sugar: 5.3g

# CRANBERRY SALAD

COOKING: 5' PREPARATION: 5' SERVES: 2

INGREDIENTS

»   1 Sugar free cranberry jello pack (1/2 cup for snacks allowed)
»   1/2 cup celery chopped (1 green)
»   7 Half Cut Walnut (1 snack)

DIRECTIONS

1. Jello mix according to the instructions of the box.
2. Attach walnuts and celery.
3. Allow setting.
4. Shake until serving.
5. Requires servings in 4-1/2 cups.

NUTRITIONS: Fats: 11 g Sodium: 73 mg Potassium: 212 mg Carbohydrates: 54 g Protein:4.1 g

# CHIA PUDDING

COOKING: 0' PREPARATION: 20' SERVES: 2

INGREDIENTS
- 4 tbsp chia seeds
- 1 cup unsweetened coconut milk
- 1/2 cup raspberries

DIRECTIONS

1. Add raspberry and coconut milk into a blender and blend until smooth.
2. Pour mixture into the glass jar.
3. Add chia seeds in a jar and stir well.
4. Seal the jar with a lid and shake well and place in the
refrigerator for 3 hours.
5. Serve chilled and enjoy.

NUTRITIONS: Calories: 360 Fat: 33 g Carbs: 13 g Sugar: 5 g Protein: 6 g Cholesterol:0 mg

# AVOCADO PUDDING

COOKING: 0' PREPARATION: 20' SERVES: 8

INGREDIENTS

- 2 ripe avocados, pitted and cut into pieces
- 1 tbsp fresh lime juice
- 14 oz can coconut milk
- 2 tsp liquid stevia
- 2 tsp vanilla

DIRECTIONS

1. Inside the blender Add all ingredients and blend until smooth.
2. Serve immediately and enjoy.

NUTRITIONS: Calories: 317 Fat: 30 g Carbs: 9 g Sugar: 0.5 g Protein: 3 g Cholesterol:0 mg

# RASPBERRY ICE CREAM

COOKING: 0' PREPARATION: 10' SERVES: 2

INGREDIENTS

- 1 cup frozen raspberries
- 1/2 cup heavy cream
- 1/8 tsp stevia powder

DIRECTIONS

1. Blend all the listed ingredients in a blender until smooth.
2. Serve immediately and enjoy.

NUTRITIONS: Calories: 144 Fat: 11 g Carbs: 10 g Sugar: 4 g Protein: 2 g Cholesterol: 41 mg

www.ingramcontent.com/pod-product-compliance
Lightning Source LLC
Chambersburg PA
CBHW071529080526
44588CB00011B/1602